# 30-DAY
# SEEKING
# WISDOM
## *Journal*

Design and distribution by Bublish, Inc.
ISBN: 979-8-89989-051-2 (eBook)
ISBN: 979-8-89989-053-6 (paperback)
ISBN: 979-8-89989-554-8 (hardcover)
ISBN: 979-8-89989-054-3 (audiobook)

# Acknowledgments

*With a heart full of gratitude, I dedicate this journal to the men and my mother who have consistently been a source of strength, wisdom, and unconditional love in my life.*

*To my incredible husband, Kevin — thank you for walking beside me with unwavering support, patience, and encouragement. Your steadfast faith and love are a true reflection of God's grace in my life. I am blessed to do life and purpose with you.*

*To our amazing sons, Daniel, Isaiah, and Malachi — you inspire me every single day. Your curiosity, compassion, and growth remind me of the importance of seeking wisdom and walking boldly in truth. You are my legacy and my motivation.*

*To my beloved stepfather, Johnny Hall — thank you for your quiet strength, your kind heart, and the steady example you have set over the years. Your presence in my life has been a gift from God.*

*And to my beautiful mother, Trifonia — thank you for planting the seeds of faith and resilience in me. Your prayers, love, and example have been foundational, and I honor you deeply.*

*May this journal serve as a reflection of the wisdom, love, and guidance I've been blessed to receive, and may it encourage others to seek God's voice in every season of life.*
*With all my love,*

# Table of Contents

"For wisdom is a defence,
and money is a defence:
but the excellency of
knowledge is, that
wisdom giveth life to
them that have it."

Ecclesiastes 7:12 (KJV)

# The Beginning of Wisdom

*Proverbs 1:7(KJV)– "The fear of the Lord is the beginning of knowledge: but fools despise wisdom and instruction."*

## Morning Prayer
*Heavenly Father,*
*Today I rise with a heart open to receive Your wisdom. Guide my thoughts, order my steps, and let Your Spirit lead me into deeper understanding. Teach me to fear You in reverence and love, and to embrace Your instruction. Give me a discerning heart and a teachable spirit. I surrender this day to Your will and ask for divine insight.*
*In Jesus' name, Amen.*

## Fasting Focus
(6:00 AM – 12:00 PM) Fast from food, media, or another distraction that pulls you from time with God. Use this time for spiritual clarity and reflection.

## Prayer Focus During Fasting:

- Ask God to reveal any areas of pride or resistance to instruction.
- Pray for a renewed hunger for His Word and guidance.
- Intercede for someone in need of divine wisdom.

## Midday Wisdom Reflection
Pause and reread Proverbs 1:7.
Ask yourself:
- Do I fear the Lord in my daily decisions?
- Am I inviting or resisting instruction?

## Journaling Prompts
- What do I need wisdom for today?
- Am I truly expecting God to answer?
- What area do I often try to figure out on my own?
- What wisdom has God already given that I haven't applied?

## Evening Reflection
Reread the scripture. Quiet your spirit and allow God to speak. Reflect on how you walked in wisdom today or where you struggled.

## Nightly Prayer

*Father God,*
*As this day comes to a close, I thank You for walking with me and for every moment of learning. Forgive me for the times I leaned on my own understanding. Continue to teach me to seek Your wisdom above all. Help me rest tonight with peace and assurance that You are molding me into a wise and faithful servant.*
*In Jesus' name, Amen.*

# Ask for Wisdom

*James 1:5 (KJV) – "If any of you lack wisdom, let him ask of God, that giveth to all men liberally, and upbraideth not; and it shall be given him."*

## Morning Prayer

*Lord, today I come boldly before Your throne and ask for wisdom. I trust Your promise that You will give freely to those who ask. Open my heart to receive without doubting. Let Your wisdom guide me through decisions, conversations, and challenges. Thank You for being generous and patient with me.*
*In Jesus' name, Amen.*

## Fasting Focus
(6:00 AM – 12:00 PM)
Fast from self-reliance. Spend time praying over situations where you usually rely on your own understanding.

## Prayer Focus During Fasting:

- Ask God to fill every decision with His insight.
- Pray against double-mindedness.
- Commit your thoughts to the Lord.

## Midday Wisdom Reflection
Pause and reread James 1:5.
Ask yourself:
- Am I truly asking for wisdom in faith?
- Where do I doubt God's willingness to lead me?

## Journaling Prompts
- What do I need wisdom for today?
- Am I truly expecting God to answer?
- What area do I often try to figure out on my own?
- What wisdom has God already given that I haven't applied?

## Evening Reflection
Reread the scripture. Invite God to show you where He provided wisdom today.

## Nightly Prayer

*God of Wisdom, Thank You for hearing me when I called out for guidance. Even when I didn't see immediate answers, I believe You are working in wisdom on my behalf. Help me rest tonight with confidence in Your generous heart. Amen.*

# Trust His Ways

*Proverbs3:5-6 (KJV) – "Trustin theLord with all thine heart; and lean not unto thine own understanding. In all thy ways acknowledge him, and he shall direct thy paths."*

## Morning Prayer
*Father,*
*I lay down my assumptions and control. I want to trust You with my whole heart. Help me not to lean on my own understanding today. I acknowledge You in every plan, every step, and every moment. Lead me in the way I should go.*
*In Jesus' name, Amen.*

## Fasting Focus
(6:00 AM – 12:00 PM)
Fast from negative self-talk and doubt. Replace each thought with trust declarations.

## Prayer Focus During Fasting:

- Ask for courage to release control.
- Pray for direction in unclear areas.
- Thank God for being trustworthy.

## Midday Wisdom Reflection
Pause and reread Proverbs 3:5-6.
Ask yourself:
- Am I trusting God fully today?
- Where have I leaned on my own understanding?

## Journaling Prompts
- Where have I been leaning on my own understanding?
- How can I acknowledge God more today?
- What does it look like to trust God with all my heart?
- How has God proven trustworthy in the past?

## Evening Reflection
Reflect on your decisions and moments of trust today.
How did God direct your steps?

## Nightly Prayer

*Lord,*
*You are faithful and true. Thank You for directing my steps today. Help me continue to trust You tomorrow and beyond. Even when things are unclear, I choose to believe that You are leading me with love and purpose.*
*Amen.*

# Wisdom in the Waiting

*Psalm 27:14 (KJV)–"Wait on the Lord:be of good courage, and he shall strengthen thine heart: wait, I say, on the Lord."*

## Morning Prayer
*God of Patience, Waiting is hard, but I know that Your timing is perfect. Teach me to wait with courage and hope. Strengthen my heart today and show me the value in this season. May I find joy in the process of becoming wise through waiting. Amen.*

## Fasting Focus
(6:00 AM – 12:00 PM)
Fast from impatience. Be mindful in small delays and practice stillness.

## Prayer Focus During Fasting:

- Ask for strength during seasons of waiting.
- Pray for renewed courage.
- Reflect on the purpose in waiting.

## Midday Wisdom Reflection
Pause and reread Psalm 27:14.
Ask yourself:
- Am I waiting with courage or frustration?
- How has God strengthened me today?

## Journaling Prompts
- What am I waiting on God for right now?
- How am I growing in the waiting?
- What does courage look like during a waiting season?
- Have I been resisting or embracing the wait?

## Evening Reflection
Consider how you responded to waiting moments.
Did you feel God's nearness?

## Nightly Prayer

*Father, Thank You for walking with me in the wait. Help me to see Your hand even in the silent seasons. Strengthen my heart again as I rest tonight. Let me not grow weary in well-doing. I trust You, Lord. Amen.*

# The Spirit of Wisdom

*Isaiah 11:2(KJV)–"And the spirit of the Lord shall rest upon him, the spirit of wisdom and understanding..."*

## Morning Prayer

*Heavenly Father, I invite You to rest upon me today. Fill me with wisdom and understanding that comes from heaven. Let me discern what is right and good. Lead me in truth and teach me to recognize Your voice above all others. Quiet every distraction that pulls me away from Your presence. May my thoughts, choices, and actions reflect Your heart and bring glory to Your name.*

## Fasting Focus

(6:00 AM – 12:00 PM)
Fast from confusion and double-mindedness. Declare clarity.

## Prayer Focus During Fasting:

- Welcome the Holy Spirit's guidance.
- Pray for spiritual sensitivity.
- Ask for discernment in relationships and decisions.

## Midday Wisdom Reflection

Pause and reread Isaiah 11:2.
Ask yourself:
- Where have I sensed the Spirit's guidance today?
- How has wisdom shaped my decisions so far?

## Journaling Prompts

- How do I experience the Holy Spirit in daily life?
- What is the Spirit saying to me today?
- Where do I need more spiritual understanding?
- How can I grow more sensitive to God's voice?

## Evening Reflection

Review the ways you noticed or missed the Spirit's prompting.

## Nightly Prayer

*Spirit of Truth,
Thank You for Your presence today. Help me to stay attuned to Your leading. Let me dream dreams inspired by heaven and wake with renewed wisdom. Cover me tonight with Your peace.
Amen.*

# Walking in Wisdom

*Ephesians5:15-16 (KJV) – "See then that ye walk circumspectly, not as fools, but as wise, redeeming the time,becausethe days are evil."*

## Morning Prayer
*Lord, teach me to walk wisely today.*
*Let me use my time well and be intentional in all I do. Help me to be alert and aware of what You are doing around me. May I live with purpose and wisdom.*
*Remind me that each moment is a gift and every decision an opportunity to honor You. Shape my heart to seek wisdom above convenience.*

## Fasting Focus
(6:00 AM – 12:00 PM)
Fast from distraction. Stay present and focused during prayer, work, and rest.

## Prayer Focus During Fasting:

- Pray for time management and discernment.
- Ask to walk in alignment with God's plan.
- Reflect on how to live wisely in today's world.

## Midday Wisdom Reflection
Pause and reread Ephesians 5:15-16.
Ask yourself:
- Am I walking with purpose today?
- How have I redeemed time or wasted it?

## Journaling Prompts
- What distractions keep me from walking wisely?
- How can I redeem my time better?
- Am I walking with purpose?
- Where do I see foolishness around or within me?

## Evening Reflection
Reflect on how you used your time and focus. Did you walk wisely?

## Nightly Prayer

*Wise God,*
*Thank You for guiding my steps today. Forgive me for time wasted or misused. Show me how to walk in greater wisdom tomorrow. Help me to be a light in dark times. I rest in Your instruction.*
*Amen.*

# Speak with Wisdom

*Proverbs 18:21(KJV)–"Death and life are in the power of the tongue: and they that love it shall eat the fruit thereof."*

## Morning Prayer

*Lord, set a guard over my mouth. Let my words today be wise, kind, and life-giving. Teach me to speak with purpose and clarity. May I use my voice to glorify You and edify others. Remind me that words have power, help me to choose mine with grace. Let every conversation reflect Your heart and truth. Amen.*

## Fasting Focus
(6:00 AM – 12:00 PM)
Fast from gossip, negativity, and idle talk. Practice speaking only what is uplifting.

## Prayer Focus During Fasting:

- Ask God to purify your speech.
- Pray for words that heal and restore.
- Speak blessings over yourself and others.

## Midday Wisdom Reflection

Pause and reread Proverbs 18:21.
Ask yourself:
- What fruit have my words produced today?
- Did I speak life or something less?

## Journaling Prompts
- What kind of words did I speak today?
- How can my words carry more wisdom?
- Who needs to hear life-giving words from me?
- What is God teaching me about my speech?

## Evening Reflection

Think over your conversations. What could've been said differently?

## Nightly Prayer

*Father,*
*Thank You for the power of speech. Forgive me for careless words. Help me grow in wisdom with what I say and how I say it. Let me rest tonight with a heart tuned to Your truth.*
*Amen.*

# The Company You Keep

*Proverbs13:20(KJV)–"He that walketh with wise men shall be wise: but a companion of fools shall be destroyed."*

## Morning Prayer

*God, thank You for the gift of wise counsel. Help me choose my relationships wisely. Bring mentors, friends, and community that sharpen and uplift me. Remove any influence that leads me away from wisdom. Give me discernment to recognize voices that reflect Your truth, and courage to walk away from those that don't. May I always be humble enough to listen and wise enough to apply what I've received. Amen.*

## Fasting Focus
(6:00 AM – 12:00 PM)
Fast from unhealthy connections (social media, toxic influences). Pray for discernment.

## Prayer Focus During Fasting:

- Ask God to reveal wise and unwise influences.
- Pray for strong, godly connections.
- Reflect on how your circle impacts your wisdom walk.

## Midday Wisdom Reflection
Pause and reread Proverbs 13:20.
Ask yourself:
- Who has the strongest influence on me?
- Are they drawing me closer to wisdom or pulling me away?

## Journaling Prompts
- Who influences me the most right now?
- Am I surrounding myself with wise counsel?
- What friendships help or hinder my growth?
- How can I become a wise companion to others?

## Evening Reflection
Consider your community. Are you growing in wisdom through them?

## Nightly Prayer

*Wise and Sovereign God,
Thank You for placing the right people in my life. Help me to be wise in my associations. Protect me from foolish influence and teach me to grow in community. I rest tonight under Your guidance and grace.
Amen.*

# Wise in Heart

*Proverbs 16:21(KJV)–"The wise in heart shall be called prudent: and the sweetness of the lips increaseth learning."*

## Morning Prayer

*Lord, create in me a wise heart. Let my words and actions reflect prudence, patience, and kindness. May my speech inspire learning and my presence bring peace. Help me grow into someone who carries wisdom with humility. Teach me to listen more than I speak and to discern what is right in every situation. May Your wisdom shine through me, drawing others closer to You. Amen.*

## Fasting Focus

(6:00 AM – 12:00 PM)
Fast from impulsiveness, pause before responding or acting. Choose thoughtful, Spirit-led responses.

## Prayer Focus During Fasting:

- Ask God to develop a wise heart in you.
- Pray for prudence in all your decisions.
- Seek wisdom in how you communicate with others.

## Midday Wisdom Reflection

Pause and reread Proverbs 16:21.
Ask yourself:
- What am I speaking from today, wisdom or impulse?
- Where have I modeled prudence?

## Journaling Prompts

- What does it mean to have a "wise heart"?
- How can I grow in prudence today?
- Have I used my words to teach or uplift?
- What emotions or situations challenge my wisdom?

## Evening Reflection

Recall a moment you responded with a wise heart. Or one where you didn't.

## Nightly Prayer

*Father,*
*thank You for the lessons today. Forgive me for moments when I was quick to speak or slow to listen. Make me a vessel of wise words and a reflection of Your heart.*
*Amen.*

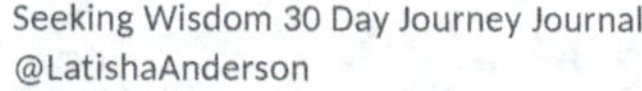

# Journal

# God's Wisdom vs. Worldly Wisdom

*1 Corinthians 3:19 (KJV) – "For the wisdom of this world is foolishness with God..."*

## Morning Prayer

*Heavenly Father, I want to be led by Your wisdom, not the opinions or patterns of this world. Give me discernment to recognize the difference. Let Your truth be louder than cultural noise. Train my heart to value eternal principles over temporary trends. Make me wise, not in the eyes of men, but in the fear and knowledge of You. Amen.*

## Fasting Focus

(6:00 AM – 12:00 PM)
Fast from popular voices or media that contradict God's truth.

## Prayer Focus During Fasting:

- Ask God to help you discern what is truly wise.
- Pray for boldness to reject worldly wisdom.
- Ask for clarity when the world's wisdom seems appealing.

## Midday Wisdom Reflection

Pause and reread 1 Corinthians 3:19.
Ask yourself:
- Have I followed worldly wisdom today?
- Where is God calling me to think differently?

## Journaling Prompts

- Where have I unknowingly embraced worldly thinking?
- What is one truth from God's Word that challenges culture?
- How can I renew my mind with godly wisdom today?
- What areas require me to take a stand for God's truth?

## Evening Reflection

Think about decisions today, were they shaped by God or culture?

## Nightly Prayer

*God of Truth,*
*cleanse my mind from worldly influence. Let me be renewed by Your Word and confident in Your wisdom. I rest tonight in the safety of Your truth.*
*Amen.*

# Journal

# Wisdom and Obedience

*Matthew 7:24 (KJV)–"Therefore whosoever heareth these sayings of mine, and doeth them, I will liken himunto a wise man..."*

## Morning Prayer

*Lord, I don't want to just hear Your Word, I want to live it. Teach me to walk in obedience today. Show me where I can apply Your truth, even when it's hard. Strengthen my spirit to follow through with faith and courage. Amen.*

## Fasting Focus

(6:00 AM – 12:00 PM)
Fast from selective obedience. Commit to follow through, even in small things.

## Prayer Focus During Fasting:

- Pray for strength to obey God's Word fully.
- Ask for help in areas where obedience is hard.
- Reflect on past moments of disobedience and seek grace.

## Midday Wisdom Reflection

Pause and reread Matthew 7:24.
Ask yourself:
- Am I hearing God's Word but not doing it?
- What small act of obedience is God prompting me toward today?

## Journaling Prompts

- Is there something God asked me to do that I've delayed?
- How does obedience reflect wisdom?
- What blessing might be waiting on the other side of obedience?
- How do I feel when I walk in obedience?

## Evening Reflection

Think about a moment today when you chose obedience, even when it was hard.

## Nightly Prayer

*Father,*
*Thank You for Your Word.*
*Help me to be a doer and not just a hearer.*
*Forgive me for the times I hesitated or ignored Your instruction.*
*I want to build my life on a firm foundation of obedience and truth.*
*Let my actions honor You and reflect a heart that trusts You completely.*
*Amen.*

# Wisdom in Correction

*Proverbs 9:8-9 (KJV)–"Rebuke a wiseman, and he will love thee. Give instruction to a wise man, and he will be yet wiser…"*

## Morning Prayer

*Lord, Help me to embrace correction. Let my heart be soft and teachable. Thank You for the people You place in my life to guide me. Use correction to shape me into the person You've called me to be. Remind me that discipline is a sign of Your love and a path to deeper wisdom. May I welcome Your refining hand, knowing it draws me closer to Your will. Amen.*

## Fasting Focus
(6:00 AM – 12:00 PM)
Fast from defensiveness or pride when being corrected.

## Prayer FocusDuringFasting:
- Pray for humility to receive correction.
- Ask God to show you areas that need refining.
- Thank Him for those who speak truth into your life.

## Midday Wisdom Reflection

Pause and reread Proverbs 9:8-9.
Let this scripture settle into your heart.
Ask yourself:
- Do I respond to correction with love and gratitude— or with resistance?
- What can I learn today that will make me wiser?
- Am I surrounding myself with people who help refine me?

## Journaling Prompts
- How do I typically respond to correction?
- When was the last time correction made me wiser?
- Who holds me accountable in love?
- What has God corrected in me recently?

## Evening Reflection

Recall how Scripture shaped your responses and choices today.

## Nightly Prayer

*Gracious God,
thank You for loving me enough to correct me. Help me embrace instruction with gratitude. May I grow in grace and wisdom with every lesson You teach.
Amen.*

# Wisdom and Peace

*James3:17(KJV)–"But the wisdom that is from above is first pure, then peaceable..."*

### Morning Prayer

*Lord, let Your peace guide my heart today. Help me respond with gentleness and wisdom in all situations. May my decisions be rooted in peace, not panic or pride. Remind me that true wisdom is calm, steady, and full of mercy. Let Your presence quiet every anxious thought as I walk in step with You. Amen.*

### Fasting Focus

(6:00 AM – 12:00 PM)
Fast from internal chaos—practice inner stillness and peaceful responses.

### Prayer Focus During Fasting:

- Ask for wisdom that brings peace.
- Pray against anxiety or strife.
- Speak peace over situations in your life.

### Midday Wisdom Reflection

Pause and reread James 3:17.
Ask yourself:
- Is my pursuit of wisdom marked by peace and purity?
- Am I allowing God's wisdom to settle anxious thoughts and calm my spirit?

### Journaling Prompts

- How do I recognize peace in my decisions?
- What situations disturb my inner peace?
- How can I bring peace into my home, work, or relationships?
- How is peace connected to wisdom?

### Evening Reflection

Look back on your day. Did peace guide your decisions? Consider how God's wisdom invited you to respond gently, with purity of heart. Thank Him for His calming presence and truth.

### Nightly Prayer

*Prince of Peace,
thank You for calming my heart. I want to walk in the kind of wisdom that produces peace and unity. Let my rest tonight be filled with stillness and security in You.
Amen.*

# Journal

# Seek Wise Counsel

*Proverbs 11:14(KJV)–"Where no counsel is, the people fall: but in the multitude of counsellors there is safety."*

### Morning Prayer
*Father, Surround me with godly counsel. Help me not to isolate myself or rely solely on my own opinions. Lead me to mentors and voices who speak with wisdom and truth. Remind me that safety and clarity are often found in the guidance of others. Give me the humility to listen and the discernment to receive what aligns with Your Word. Amen.*

### Fasting Focus
(6:00 AM – 12:00 PM)
Fast from isolation or stubborn independence. Reach out for insight.

### Prayer Focus During Fasting:

- Ask for humility to seek help.
- Pray for clarity about who should speak into your life.
- Intercede for your spiritual leaders and mentors.

### Midday Wisdom Reflection
Pause and consider:
Am I seeking advice or relying solely on myself?
Who are the godly people I can turn to for wise counsel today?

### Journaling Prompts
- Do I have a circle of wise counsel?
- Who do I go to when I need advice?
- What makes someone a wise counselor?
- How have I benefited from godly mentorship?

### Evening Reflection
Reflect on how you handled decisions today. Did you invite godly wisdom from others? Thank God for the people He has placed around you who guide you with truth and love.

### Nightly Prayer

*Lord, thank You for those You've placed in my life to guide and counsel me. Help me be open to wise voices and closed off to foolish ones. Cover my decisions with safety through counsel. Amen.*

*Journal*

# The Rewards of Wisdom

*Proverbs 3:13-14(KJV) – "Happy is the man that findeth wisdom... for the merchandise of it is better than the merchandise of silver..."*

## Morning Prayer

*Thank You, Lord, for the treasure that is wisdom. Help me to value it more than riches or recognition. Let my life reflect the joy and reward of walking in Your truth. May I never take Your guidance for granted, and may Your wisdom continually shape my decisions, my character, and my legacy.*

## Fasting Focus
(6:00 AM – 12:00 PM)
Fast from comparing material success. Focus on eternal rewards.

## Prayer Focus During Fasting:

- Thank God for the joy of walking in wisdom.
- Pray to value spiritual growth over material gain.
- Reflect on what wisdom has already brought to your life.

## Midday Wisdom Reflection
Ask yourself:
- Am I valuing wisdom more than temporary gain?
- What spiritual reward has come from a wise choice recently?

## Journaling Prompts
- What blessings have I experienced from choosing wisdom?
- How does wisdom bring joy?
- What worldly treasures have distracted me from godly wisdom?
- How can I share the reward of wisdom with others?

## Evening Reflection

Reflect on moments where you chose wisdom over quick success. Celebrate the inner joy and long-term fruit it brings. Thank God for wisdom that is eternal and life-giving.

## Nightly Prayer

*God,*
*You are the greatest treasure. I thank You for every reward that comes from walking in wisdom. Keep my heart anchored in Your truth and help me sleep in contentment tonight.*
*Amen.*

# Journal

# Wisdom from Experience

*Romans5:3-4(KJV) – "Tribulation worketh patience; and patience, experience; and experience, hope."*

## Morning Prayer

*God,*
*I thank You for every lesson hidden in difficulty. Help me to see how You use trials to teach and shape me. Remind me that nothing is wasted in Your hands and that every hardship holds a purpose. May I learn from experience and grow stronger in hope. Amen.*

## Fasting Focus
(6:00 AM – 12:00 PM)
Fast from complaining about past experiences. Reflect with gratitude.

## Prayer Focus During Fasting:

- Thank God for growth through trials.
- Ask Him to help you see with spiritual perspective.
- Pray for someone learning through hardship.

## Midday Wisdom Reflection
Ask yourself:
- What current trial is building experience and hope in me?
- How has God used past struggles to mature me?

## Journaling Prompts
- What past experience taught me deep wisdom?
- How has God used trials for my good?
- What patterns have I repeated that I need to release?
- How can I turn past lessons into present growth?

## Evening Reflection
Tonight, reflect on how your trials have shaped you. Thank God for turning tribulation into wisdom and experience into unshakable hope.

## Nightly Prayer

*Lord, thank You for the journey. Even when it's been painful, You've been present. I trust that nothing is wasted. Let the wisdom I've gained become seeds of hope for tomorrow.*
*Amen.*

# Journal

# Boldness in Wisdom

*2Timothy1:7(KJV)–"For God hath not given us the spirit of fear; but of power, and of love, and of a sound mind."*

## Morning Prayer

*Lord, today I walk in boldness.*
*I reject fear and embrace the sound mind You've given me. Let wisdom lead me with courage and faith. I am empowered by Your Spirit. Strengthen me to speak truth with love and to act with confidence rooted in You. May every step reflect Your power at work within me. Amen.*

## Fasting Focus
(6:00 AM – 12:00 PM)
Fast from fear-based thinking. Declare bold faith.

## Prayer FocusDuringFasting:
- Pray for courage to make wise decisions.
- Ask God to calm anxious thoughts.
- Declare God's power in every area of life.

## Midday Wisdom Reflection
Ask yourself:
- Am I acting from fear or from faith today?
- How can I walk in bold, Spirit-led wisdom?

## Journaling Prompts
- Where is fear blocking my wisdom?
- How can I walk in boldness today?
- What does a sound mind look like in this season?
- What courageous step is God asking me to take?

## Evening Reflection
Review your steps today. Were they hesitant or bold in the Lord? Give thanks for the Spirit of power and sound mind, and ask for courage to walk in truth tomorrow.

## Nightly Prayer

*Father, thank You for the boldness You placed within me. Help me to use it with wisdom, not pride. May I rest knowing that You've equipped me for every challenge.*
*Amen.*

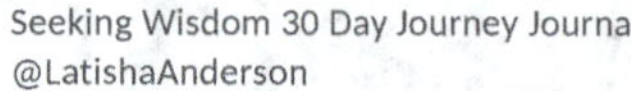

# Wisdom in Planning

*Proverbs21:5(KJV)–"The thoughts of the diligent tend only to plenteousness..."*

### Morning Prayer

*Lord, order my thoughts and help me plan with wisdom. Let me not move impulsively but be diligent and strategic. I trust You to guide my steps with purpose.*
*Remind me that success begins with seeking You first. May every plan I make be surrendered to Your will.*
*Amen.*

### Fasting Focus
(6:00 AM – 12:00 PM)
Fast from procrastination. Use this time to focus and organize.

### Prayer Focus During Fasting:

- Pray for vision and direction.
- Ask for clarity in your goals.
- Submit your plans to God.

### Midday Wisdom Reflection
Ask yourself:
- Are my plans aligned with God's wisdom?
- What does diligence look like in this season?

### Journaling Prompts
- Where do I need more diligence?
- How can I plan better with God's wisdom?
- What vision is God placing before me?
- How have poor plans impacted my progress?

### Evening Reflection

Examine your day's plans and actions. Were they thoughtful and purposeful? Thank God for guiding your steps, and trust Him to bless the plans surrendered to Him.

### Nightly Prayer

*Wise God, thank You for clarity today. As I sleep, renew my vision and remind me of the diligence needed to walk it out. I trust in Your plan.*
*Amen.*

# Journal

# Wisdom to Let Go

*Ecclesiastes3:6(KJV)–"A time to get, and a time to lose; a time to keep, and a time to cast away."*

## Morning Prayer

*God, give me wisdom to know what to release. Help me let go of what no longer serves Your purpose. I trust You to bring new things as I make space for Your will. Remind me that letting go is not losing, but making room for Your greater plan. Strengthen my heart to surrender fully, knowing You are faithful.*
*Amen.*

## Fasting Focus
(6:00 AM – 12:00 PM)
Fast from holding on to things God is asking you to release.

## Prayer Focus During Fasting:

- Ask God what needs to be let go.
- Pray for peace and closure.
- Declare freedom from old weights.

## Midday Wisdom Reflection
Ask yourself:
- What am I holding onto that God is asking me to release?
- Do I trust Him with both gain and loss?

## Journaling Prompts
- What is God asking me to release?
- Why have I been holding on to it?
- What freedom could come from letting go?
- How does letting go lead to wisdom?

## Evening Reflection

Reflect on what you may have released today: an expectation, a habit, or control. Let peace settle in your heart, knowing God holds what you've let go.

## Nightly Prayer

*Lord, thank You for giving and taking away with wisdom. I release all that hinders. May I rest in freedom, knowing that You are in control. Amen.*

# Wisdom and Discernment

*Hebrews5:14(KJV)– "...by reason of use have their senses exercised to discern both good and evil."*

## Morning Prayer

*Holy Spirit, sharpen my discernment today. Help me see beneath the surface. Let me not judge by appearance but be led by truth and insight. Expose anything false that appears good, and reveal what is truly from You even if it comes in unexpected ways. Teach me to listen closely and respond with wisdom, not impulse. Amen.*

## Fasting Focus
(6:00 AM – 12:00 PM)
Fast from assumptions. Seek clarity before conclusions.

## Prayer FocusDuringFasting:
- Ask for discernment in relationships.
- Pray for spiritual sensitivity.
- Reflect on past moments of misjudgment.

## Midday Wisdom Reflection
Ask yourself:
- Am I practicing spiritual discernment?
- What decisions today required wisdom to distinguish right from wrong?

## Journaling Prompts
- Where do I need greater discernment?
- What decisions require spiritual insight?
- How do I practice using discernment daily?
- What have I learned from poor judgment?

## Evening Reflection

As you reflect, were your senses trained by the Word? Thank God for sharpening your discernment and guiding you toward what is good.

## Nightly Prayer

*Lord, thank You for revealing truth today. Help me continue to grow in discernment, walking in wisdom and grace. Amen.*

# Journal

# Wisdom in Transition

*Isaiah43:19(KJV)-"Behold,I will do a new thing; now it shall spring forth; shall ye not know it?"*

## Morning Prayer

*Lord, I thank You for new beginnings. Give me the wisdom to navigate this transition season with grace and boldness. Help me release what was and embrace what is becoming. Make my steps firm and full of faith. Let Your Spirit lead me when the path is unfamiliar, and remind me that You are doing a new thing for my good. I choose to trust You with what's next, knowing You are already there.*

## Fasting Focus
(6:00 AM – 12:00 PM)
Fast from fear of change. Say no to second-guessing, and yes to forward movement.

## Prayer Focus During Fasting:

Ask for discernment in relationships.
Pray for spiritual sensitivity.
Reflect on past moments of misjudgment.

## Midday Wisdom Reflection

Ask yourself:

- Am I perceiving the new thing God is doing?
- How can I lean into His plans rather than resist change?

## Journaling Prompts

What transitions are you currently facing?
Where do you need wisdom to let go, shift, or step into something new?

## Evening Reflection

Reflect on any new beginnings, opportunities, or endings today. Thank God for faithfully leading you through transitions with wisdom and grace.

## Nightly Prayer

*Faithful Father,
Thank You for walking with me through this season of change. Even when the path is unfamiliar, I trust that You are leading me. Give me peace tonight and assurance that You are doing a new thing in my life. Help me rest knowing that transition is part of transformation.
In Jesus' name, Amen.*

# Journal

# Wisdom in Your Relationships

*"If it is possible, as far as it depends on you, live at peace with everyone." –Romans 12:18 (NIV)*

## Morning Prayer

*Lord, give me wisdom in my interactions. Let my words bring healing, not harm. Show me how to pursue peace even when it's difficult. Teach me to listen before I speak, and to respond with grace even when I am challenged. May my presence reflect Your love and wisdom in every conversation. Amen.*

## Fasting Focus
(6:00 AM – 12:00 PM)
Fast from unhealthy conversations or social media today. Pray for God to reveal wisdom in how you approach your relationships, both new and old.

## Prayer Focus During Fasting:

- Ask for discernment in relationships.
- Pray for spiritual sensitivity.
- Reflect on past moments of misjudgment.

## Midday Wisdom Reflection
Ask yourself:
- Am I pursuing peace or fueling conflict?
- What relationship needs wisdom and grace right now?

## Journaling Prompts
- Where do I need to seek peace in a relationship?
- How has wisdom helped me navigate conflict in the past?

## Evening Reflection
Consider your interactions today. Did you strive for peace? Thank God for teaching you to respond with humility, love, and understanding.

## Nightly Prayer

*Lord, thank You for revealing truth today. Help me continue to grow in discernment, walking in wisdom and grace. Amen.*

# Wisdom to Finish Strong

*2Timothy4:7(KJV)–"I have fought a good fight, I have finished my course, I have kept the faith."*

## Morning Prayer

*Lord, give me the strength and wisdom to finish what You have started in me. Help me stay focused and faithful until the end. I declare that I will run my race with endurance and purpose, keeping my eyes on You. Strengthen me when I feel weary, and remind me that Your grace is sufficient for every step. May my life bring glory to You as I complete the work You've entrusted to me.*
*Amen.*

## Fasting Focus
(6:00 AM – 12:00 PM)
Fast from laziness and procrastination. Commit your time to God's priorities.

## Prayer Focus During Fasting:

- Pray for endurance in your spiritual and personal journey.
- Ask God to renew your energy for the tasks ahead.
- Declare victory over distractions and discouragement.

## Midday Wisdom Reflection

Ask yourself:
- Am I persevering or growing weary?
- What will finishing strong look like today?

## Journaling Prompts
- Where do I need wisdom to finish well?
- What "race" or assignment is God calling me to complete?
- What is holding me back from pressing forward?
- How has God helped me stay the course?

## Evening Reflection

As you close the day, did you remain faithful in the little things? Thank God for endurance and ask Him to strengthen you to finish every assignment well.

## Nightly Prayer

*Lord, thank You for strengthening me today. I trust that what You've begun, You will finish. Help me to keep the faith no matter what. Let me rest knowing I am one step closer to fulfilling my purpose.*
*Amen.*

# Wise Counsel

*Proverbs 11:14(KJV)–"Where no counsel is, the people fall: but in the multitude of counsellors there is safety."*

## Morning Prayer

*Father, guide me to wise and godly counsel. Help me be humble enough to receive advice and discern those You've sent to speak into my life. Protect me from misleading voices and keep me rooted in Your truth.*
*Amen.*

## Fasting Focus
(6:00 AM – 12:00 PM)
Fast from making decisions without prayer or counsel.

## Prayer FocusDuringFasting:
- Ask God to send you godly mentors and advisors.
- Pray for discernment in choosing who to trust.
- Thank God for past wisdom received through others.

## Midday Wisdom Reflection
Pause and consider:
- Have I sought wise counsel today or leaned on my own understanding?
- Who has God placed in my life to offer godly wisdom and guidance?
- Am I open to correction and insight from others?

## Journaling Prompts
- Who are the voices of wisdom in my life right now?
- How open am I to correction or counsel?
- What decisions do I need help with?
- How has godly counsel saved me from error?

## Evening Reflection
Look back on any decisions, conversations, or thoughts from today. Did you seek out or listen to godly advice? Thank God for the people He uses to protect and guide you through wise counsel. Ask for discernment to recognize when He is speaking through others and the humility to receive it.

## Nightly Prayer

*Lord, thank You for the people You've placed in my life to guide me. Help me recognize wisdom when it speaks and walk in humility as I grow.*
*Amen.*

# *Journal*

# The Humble Receive Wisdom

*Proverbs11:2(KJV)–"When pride cometh, then cometh shame: but with the lowly is wisdom."*

## Morning Prayer

*Lord, I humble myself before You today. Remove pride from my heart and teach me to walk in humility. I want to be teachable, gentle, and wise in every way. Lead me in meekness and strength. Let my life reflect Your wisdom through quiet obedience and a surrendered heart. May others see Your grace at work in me as I choose humility daily.*
*Amen.*

## Fasting Focus
(6:00 AM – 12:00 PM)
Fast from self-importance or being overly opinionated.

## Prayer FocusDuringFasting:
- Ask God to reveal areas of pride.
- Pray for a heart that listens before it speaks.
- Declare your dependence on God for wisdom.

## Midday Wisdom Reflection
Ask yourself:
- Am I choosing humility today?
- What lesson is God teaching me through surrender?

## Journaling Prompts
- How does humility open the door to wisdom?
- Where has pride blocked my growth?
- What does true humility look like in action?
- Who in my life models humble wisdom?

## Evening Reflection

Reflect on any moments of pride or humility. Thank God for the quiet strength found in lowliness and the wisdom He gives to the humble.

## Nightly Prayer

*Father, thank You for the gentle reminders to stay humble. I choose humility over pride. Grow wisdom in me through a soft and yielded heart.*
*Amen.*

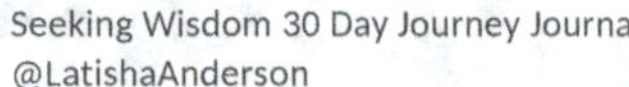

*Journal*

# Wisdom in Leadership

*Matthew20:26(KJV)–"...who so ever will be great among you, let him be your minister."*

## Morning Prayer

*God, help me lead by serving. Whether at home, at work, or in ministry, give me wisdom to influence others with grace, humility, and strength. Teach me to lead like Jesus. May my words build up, my actions reflect Your love, and my leadership point others back to You. Let every opportunity to lead be an opportunity to serve.*
*Amen.*

## Fasting Focus
(6:00 AM – 12:00 PM)
Fast from controlling tendencies. Practice servant-hearted leadership.

## Prayer Focus During Fasting:

- Pray for wisdom in your influence and leadership roles.
- Ask God to help you lead with humility.
- Intercede for leaders in your family, church, and nation.

## Midday Wisdom Reflection

Pause and reread Matthew 20:26.
Ask yourself:
- Am I leading with a servant's heart?
- How can I uplift and serve others today?

## Journaling Prompts
- How am I leading others right now?
- What kind of leader do I want to become?
- Where do I need more wisdom as a leader?
- How can I serve while leading?

## Evening Reflection

Reflect on any opportunity you had to serve today.
Thank God for redefining greatness through humility and empowering you to lead with love.

## Nightly Prayer

*Jesus, You were the greatest servant-leader. Help me model my leadership after Yours. Let me serve others with love, clarity, and wisdom.*
*Amen.*

# Guarding the Heart

*Proverbs4:23(KJV)–"Keep thy heart with all diligence; for out of it are the issues of life."*

### Morning Prayer

*Lord, help me guard my heart today. Keep me from offense, bitterness, and fear. Fill my heart with wisdom, love, and discernment. May everything that flows from me be pleasing to You. Strengthen me to choose what is right, even when it's hard, and remind me that a pure heart leads to a peaceful life. Let my thoughts, words, and actions reflect Your truth and grace. Amen.*

### Fasting Focus
(6:00 AM – 12:00 PM)
Fast from toxic thoughts and emotional clutter.

### Prayer FocusDuringFasting:
- Ask God to purify your heart and motives.
- Pray for healing from wounds that cloud your judgment.
- Declare emotional and spiritual wholeness.

### Midday Wisdom Reflection
Pause and reread Proverbs 4:23.
Ask yourself:
- What am I allowing into my heart today?
- Is my heart aligned with truth and guarded by grace?

### Journaling Prompts
- What have I allowed into my heart that God wants to remove?
- How can I guard my heart better?
- What flows out of my heart daily—life or something else?
- What does a guarded but open heart look like?

### Evening Reflection
Examine the emotional and spiritual state of your heart tonight. Surrender anything that doesn't belong and thank God for His protection and peace.

### Nightly Prayer

*Lord, cleanse my heart again tonight. Thank You for watching over my soul. Let me rest with a renewed spirit and a guarded heart full of peace. Amen.*

# Wisdom and Peace

*James 3:17 (KJV) – "But the wisdom that is from above is first pure, then peaceable, gentle… full of mercy and good fruits…"*

### Morning Prayer

*Father, today I seek not just wisdom, but peaceful wisdom. Let Your wisdom flow through me gently, purely, and with mercy. May my presence and decisions bring peace, not conflict. Help me to be a vessel of calm in chaos, a peacemaker led by Your truth. Teach me to choose words and actions that reflect Your heart.*
*Amen.*

### Fasting Focus
(6:00 AM – 12:00 PM)
Fast from anxiety and reactive speech. Embrace stillness.

### Prayer FocusDuringFasting:
- Pray for wisdom to respond peacefully.
- Ask for calmness in your emotions and reactions.
- Declare peace over your home, mind, and relationships.

### Midday Wisdom Reflection
Pause and reread Proverbs 4:7.
Ask yourself:
- What choices today require wisdom above all?
- Am I truly valuing wisdom as the principal thing?

### Journaling Prompts
- Is my wisdom peaceable and gentle or harsh and critical?
- Where do I need to bring peace today?
- How does God's wisdom change how I handle conflict?
- What fruit is my wisdom producing?

### Evening Reflection
Did I pursue wisdom above convenience today? Where did I settle for less?

### Nightly Prayer

*Prince of Peace, thank You for stilling my heart. Help me walk with a spirit of peace and wisdom. Let my words and actions reflect Your gentleness.*
*Amen.*

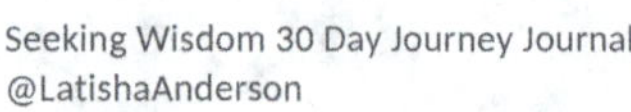

# Wisdom for the Future

*Jeremiah 29:11(KJV)–"For I know the thoughts that I think toward you, saith the Lord… to give you an expected end."*

### Morning Prayer

*Lord, I trust Your plan for my life. Give me wisdom for every next step. Help me not to rush ahead or fear the unknown, but walk with confidence in Your promises. Teach me to listen for Your voice above all others and to rest in the assurance that You go before me. Let my heart be anchored in Your peace as I follow Your lead.*
*Amen.*

### Fasting Focus
(6:00 AM – 12:00 PM)
Fast from fear about the future. Speak God's truth over your path.

### Prayer Focus During Fasting:

- Ask God to prepare you for the next season.
- Pray for peace in transition.
- Declare confidence in God's direction for your life.

### Midday Wisdom Reflection
Take a moment to pause and reflect:
- Am I trusting God's wisdom for my future, or am I trying to control the outcome?
- How can I align today's actions with the peace and purpose God has promised?

### Journaling Prompts
- What fears or doubts do I have about the future?
- Where do I need wisdom for the next step?
- How has God proven His faithfulness in the past?
- What vision or promise am I holding onto?

### Evening Reflection

As you think about tomorrow, rest in God's promises. His plans are full of hope. Thank Him for writing your story with wisdom and purpose.

### Nightly Prayer

*God of my future, thank You for having a plan for my life. I surrender my fears and dreams to You. Lead me forward in wisdom, step by step.*
*Amen.*

# The Reward of Wisdom

*Proverbs3:13(KJV)–"Happy is the man that findeth wisdom, and the man that getteth understanding."*

## Morning Prayer

*Lord, thank You for this journey of seeking wisdom. I receive the joy, strength, and reward that comes with walking in Your truth. May I continue to grow, learn, and live wisely for Your glory. Help me to never take Your guidance for granted, and may my life be a testimony of the blessings that come from Your wisdom. Keep my heart anchored in understanding and my steps steady on the path of righteousness. Amen.*

## Fasting Focus
(6:00 AM – 12:00 PM)
Fast from distraction and give thanks for what God has done this month.

## Prayer Focus During Fasting:

- Praise God for what you've learned.
- Pray for continued growth in wisdom.
- Commit to ongoing spiritual development.

## Midday Wisdom Reflection
Take a moment to reflect:
- What fruit has wisdom produced in my life recently?
- Am I recognizing the value and reward of understanding God's ways above worldly gain?

## Journaling Prompts
- How has my understanding of wisdom changed this month?
- What were the most impactful lessons?
- What will I carry forward into the next season?
- What is my commitment going forward?

## Evening Reflection

As you wind down, reflect on how the pursuit of wisdom brought peace, clarity, or joy today. Did you experience any moments where wisdom led to a better choice or outcome? Thank God for the happiness and security that come from walking in His understanding.

## Nightly Prayer

*Father, thank You for walking with me every day of this journal. Let this be the beginning of a lifelong journey of wisdom and intimacy with You. I rest in Your peace and purpose. Amen.*

"Blessed be the name of God
for ever and ever: for wisdom
and might are his... he giveth
wisdom unto the wise, and
knowledge to them that
know understanding."

Daniel 2:20-21 (KJV)

# Final Reflections:
# A Journey of Wisdom

*"Wisdom is the principal thing; therefore get wisdom: and with all thy getting get understanding." — Proverbs 4:7 (KJV)*

You've just completed a powerful 30-day journey of prayer, fasting, and seeking the wisdom of God. This was not just a spiritual exercise, it was a heart posture, a life reset, and a divine invitation to grow deeper in understanding, clarity, and truth.

Use this final space to reflect, give thanks, and prepare for what's next.

---

## 1. Gratitude and Growth

Write a few thoughts about your overall experience:
- What are you most grateful for during this 30-day journey?
- What moments were most transformational or eye-opening?
- How has your relationship with God shifted or deepened?

*My Reflection:*

## 2. Wisdom Lessons That Changed Me

Think back onthe scriptures, fasting themes,and journaling prompts.

- Which days stood out the most?
- What spiritual principles will you carry forward?
- In what area of your life have you become more wise?

Top 3 Lessons I've Learned:

### 3. Evidence of Fruit

*"By their fruit you will recognize them..."* — *Matthew 7:16*

Over 30 days, you planted seeds of discipline, humility, and discernment. Now reflect on the early fruit:

- Has your mindset changed?
- Are your decisions more prayer-led?
- Are your thoughts, words, or actions more aligned with godly wisdom?

Fruit I'm beginning to see:

## 4. Going Forward With Wisdom

*Wisdomis not a destination—it's a daily walk.*
- *What new habits or rhythms do you want to continue?*
- *What's your next spiritual focus?*
- *What has God shown you about your calling, family, business, or ministry?*

*My Commitments Beyond These 30 Days:*

"That the God of our Lord
Jesus Christ... may give
unto you the spirit of
wisdom and revelation in
the knowledge of him."

Ephesians 1:17 (KJV)

# Declaration of Wisdom

*Speak this out loud or write your own:*

I am a seeker of wisdom. I listen for God's voice and follow His lead. I am not swayed by emotions, pressure, or fear. I stand in truth. I live with intention. I walk with purpose. I walk in wisdom. I will continue to grow, serve, and lead with the understanding God gives me. I declare that wisdom will be the foundation of my life, my home, my ministry, and my legacy.

In Jesus' name, amen.

# Notes

# Notes

# Notes